LAURENCE ANHOLT has been described as "one of the most
versatile writers for children today" and was included in
The Independent On Sunday "Top 10 Children's Authors in Britain."
From his home in Lyme Regis, he has produced more than 90 children's
titles, which are published in dozens of languages around the world,
many of them in collaboration with his wife, Catherine.
His books range from the "Anholt Artists" series to the irrepressible
Chimp and Zee. Laurence has won numerous awards, including
the Nestlé Smarties Gold Award on two occasions.

Laurence and Catherine Anholt are the owners
of *Chimp and Zee, Bookshop by the Sea* in Lyme Regis.
Stocked entirely with their own signed books, prints, and cards,
and crammed with automated displays and book-related exhibits,
it is one of the most magical children's bookshops
you could ever hope to visit.

For Sylvette, who opened doors for me.

First edition for the United States, Canada, and the Philippines
published 1998 by Barron's Educational Series, Inc.

Text and illustrations © 1998 by Laurence Anholt

Picasso and the Girl With a Ponytail was conceived, edited, and produced
by Frances Lincoln Ltd., 4 Torriano Mews, Torriano Avenue,
London NW5 2RZ England

All inquiries should be addressed to:
Barron's Educational Series, Inc.
250 Wireless Boulevard
Hauppauge, New York 11788
http://www.barronseduc.com

ISBN-13: 978-0-7641-3853-9 ISBN-10: 0-7641-3853-7

The Library of Congress has catalogued the hardcover editions as follows:
Library of Congress Catalog Card No. 98-14005

Library of Congress Cataloging-in-Publication Data

Anholt, Laurence.
     Picasso and the girl with a ponytail: a story about Pablo Picasso
/ by Laurence Anholt.
     p.   cm.
     Summary: Sylvette gradually begins to gain self-confidence during
the summer she models for a renowned artist Pablo Picasso in the
French village of Vallauris.
     ISBN 0-7641-5031-6
     1. Picasso, Pablo. 1881-1973—Juvenile fiction. [1. Picasso,
Pablo. 1881-1973—Fiction. 2. Artists—Fiction.] 1. Title.
PZ7.a68635P1 1998
[Fic]-dc21   98-14005
                                                      CIP
                                                      AC
Date of manufacture: October 2012
Manufactured by: South China Printing, Dongguan, Guangdong, China

19 18 17 16 15 14 13 12 11 10 9 8 7 6 5

ACKNOWLEDGMENTS
Please note: The pages in this book are not numbered. The story begins on page 4.

Paintings and Sculptures by Pablo Picasso (1881-1973)
Front cover & Page 13: *Portrait of Sylvette David* (1954), The Art Institute of Chicago, gift of Mr. and Mrs. Leigh Block, 1955.821.
Photograph © 1998, The Art Institute of Chicago. All Rights Reserved.
Page 6 & page 27: *Portrait of Sylvette* (1954), Private Collection. Photograph Giraudon/Bridgeman Art Library
Page 12 (above): *Portrait of Sylvette* (21 April 1954, II), Musée Picasso, Paris © Photo RMN-PICASSO
Page 12 (below): *Sylvette* (1954), Kunsthalle, Bremen. Photograph Giraudon/Bridgeman Art Library
Page 17 (above left): *The Tragedy* (1903), Chester Dale Collection, National Gallery of Art, Washington. Photograph © 1998
Board of Trustees, National Gallery of Art, Washington
Page 17 (above right): *Preparatory Drawing for Guernica* (1937), Museo Nacional Centro de Arte Reina Sofia, Madrid.
Photograph Index/Bridgeman Art Library
Page 17 (below): *The Three Dancers* (1925). Photograph © Tate Gallery, London
Page 21 (left): *Baboon and Young* (1951), Musée Picasso, Paris © Photo RMN - Béatrice Hatala
Page 21 (right): *Bull's Head* (1942), Musée Picasso, Paris © Photo RMN - Béatrice Hatala
Page 26: *The Woman with a Key* (1954), Private Collection. Photograph Scala, Florence

All paintings and sculptures by Pablo Picasso copyright © Succession Picasso/DACS 1998

Pages 30-31: Photograph © François Pages *Paris-Match*

Picasso

and the
GIRL WITH A PONYTAIL

A Story about **Pablo Picasso**

by LAURENCE
ANHOLT

BARRON'S

IT WAS THE FIRST DAY OF SUMMER. Sylvette and her friends were sitting on the terrace in the sun. Sylvette was so shy that she always sat a little apart, but she listened to every word.

"Have you heard? Picasso is staying right here in Vallauris!"

"It's incredible! The most famous artist in the world. Every picture he paints is worth a fortune."

"I heard he had a huge white car sent from America, in exchange for just one painting!"

Sylvette was very interested. Secretly, she dreamed
of becoming an artist. In a suitcase under her bed was
a sketchbook full of her drawings. All her secrets
were locked inside that suitcase – things no one else
had ever seen.

Suddenly Sylvette noticed something absolutely amazing. Right in front of her eyes, a beautiful picture had appeared above the terrace wall.

"LOOK!" shouted her friends. "It's Sylvette. Only Sylvette has a ponytail like that."

Sylvette hid her face in her hands. She heard a roar of laughter from behind the wall.

They all ran to look. They saw a man holding the picture above his head. He was short, but very muscular. He wore a striped shirt, shorts, and a pair of bedroom slippers. It was Picasso!

"I saw you all from my studio," he laughed. "And I made a sketch. Come on. Why don't you visit me?"

Sylvette was last inside the door, her heart beating like a drum. The studio was a treasure house, as if the artist had never thrown away a single thing. Every surface was piled with bits and pieces – tins of paint, scraps of wood, strange sculptures, children's toys, broken pots, a cowboy hat, flowers, painted plates, a boomerang, fishbones, a clown's mask, a birdcage, guitars, a bullfighter's sword. And more than anything else, Sylvette saw paintings, hundreds and hundreds of them, each one signed with a single word: *Picasso*

Picasso was still laughing. He was 73 years old, but he acted like a young boy.

"Now then," he shouted. "I will draw one person. Who will it be?"

One of Sylvette's friends stepped forward quickly. She was very beautiful. "You can draw me, Mr. Picasso," she said. "I will sit for you."

Picasso looked at her quite fiercely. "No," he said. "You saw my picture outside. I have chosen the girl with the ponytail."

Sylvette felt a bit sick. She wanted to run straight out of the door. But Picasso was very kind. "It's all right," he said gently. "You can trust me. Come and sit down."

"Sylvette is too shy," teased her friends, "and too dreamy as well."

"That's good," laughed the artist.
"Then we will get along. Because Picasso
is a dreamer, too. Come back another
time," he called to Sylvette's friends.
"Sylvette and I have work to do."

Picasso looked carefully at Sylvette.
She was shivering.

"Here, borrow this coat," he said.
Then he began to draw.

The first drawing was slow and careful – a delicate pencil study.

The second picture was larger – Sylvette as still and nervous as a wild deer.

Then Picasso began to work faster and faster.
The pictures grew larger and more strange.
Picasso was enjoying himself.

 At the end of the day,
Sylvette ran home.

She took out her
sketchbook, but her head was spinning,
and none of her drawings came out right.

The next morning, Sylvette returned
nervously to the studio. Perhaps Picasso
had forgotten her? But he opened the door
and grinned at her like a schoolboy.

Little by little, the paintings became
more daring and more extraordinary.
Little by little, Sylvette became less shy.

Picasso seemed to change every
moment, just like his pictures. He was
as proud as a king, he painted like
a magician, and yet he liked to dress up
and play games. Sometimes he put on
funny hats or masks to make Sylvette
laugh. He told her about the animals he
had owned – dogs, a goat who was allowed
to sleep indoors, and a bad-tempered
monkey. Once he had even kept an owl.
Of course, Picasso had painted them all.

All through the summer, Picasso created pictures of Sylvette, and sculptures in cardboard and metal. As the work became bigger and bolder, she became braver, too. Sylvette's father had left home when she was small, but for that summer, Picasso was like a father to her.

Shy Sylvette with the most famous painter in the world. It was a real fairy tale.

One day, Sylvette plucked up her courage and showed Picasso her secret sketchbook. She told him about her dream of becoming an artist. Picasso didn't laugh or tease her.

"That is good," he said loudly. "But you have to be brave and learn to let go. Look at me!

When I am angry,
I make angry pictures.

When I am sad,
my pictures are sad, too,

and when I am happy,
my painting is full of joy.
Even my dreams are in
my work. There can be
no secrets in painting."

That afternoon a photographer came to the
studio. Sylvette hated having her photo taken.
She wanted to hide away. Then she saw
Picasso making funny faces at the camera,
and suddenly it didn't seem so bad.
The man took dozens of pictures of
Picasso and Sylvette beside the paintings.

Her friends couldn't believe their eyes. Shy Sylvette on the front cover of a famous magazine! And before long, every magazine wanted a picture of Picasso's new model. Girls in Paris and London were even copying her hairstyle – they all wanted a Sylvette ponytail!

Sylvette cut out all the photographs and locked them carefully in her suitcase.

Sometimes Picasso worked late into the night. Once Sylvette saw him behind the studio, in the middle of a pile of garbage, hunting for interesting objects . . . The richest artist who ever lived made sculptures from old junk.

Sylvette had seen some of them in magazines:
a baboon with two toy cars for a face, a bull's
head made from a bicycle seat and handlebars...

Sylvette loved watching Picasso work.
Paintings, sculptures, and painted pots poured
from him like a volcano.

At last Picasso started a huge sculpture of Sylvette, with old
pieces of pottery for the arms and legs. It had a long neck
and a round bag just like hers, but the head was so strange,
Sylvette didn't think it looked like her at all.

As she watched, Sylvette had a sad feeling that this would
be the last time Picasso would use her as his model.
Since the day on the terrace, she had been in his work.
Soon it would all fade like the summer.

While Picasso worked, Sylvette began telling him her secrets. She talked about the time her father had gone away. Sylvette kept a special picture of him in her suitcase, but she had never told anyone how hurt and lonely she had been.

Picasso looked up at her with burning black eyes. "It is very hard when people move apart," he said. "But try to remember – with every door that closes, a new door opens."

It began to grow dark. As they looked at the sculpture, Sylvette told Picasso a secret she had locked away and tried to forget. She talked about the man who had come to live with her mother, a loud unpleasant bully. Sylvette was sometimes so unhappy that she wanted to run away.

Picasso looked at her kindly. Then he jumped up.
"You have given me an idea," he said. "I knew something
was missing from the sculpture . . . Sylvette must hold
something in her hand!"

Picasso began searching through bits
and pieces on a table. He tipped
out a drawer onto the floor.

At last he found what he wanted.
"In her hand," Picasso announced,
"Sylvette holds . . . a key!"

He pushed a big iron key
into the hand of the sculpture.
Sylvette looked puzzled.

"She has a key because she has so many
secrets locked away." Picasso fixed the key
in place with some plaster. "But she also
has a key . . . listen, Sylvette . . . to open
new doors!"

Then Picasso reached out his hand, white with plaster, and gently touched Sylvette's face.

"Look! It is finished – The Girl with a Key. Now, Sylvette, I would like to give you a present. You may choose any picture you like. Perhaps it will help to open some doors for you."

When Sylvette stepped out of Picasso's studio for the last time, she was carrying that very first picture. She held it carefully because the paint on the signature was not quite dry – *For Sylvette, From Picasso*. A beautiful picture of The Girl with a Ponytail.

After that summer, Sylvette began to paint as bravely as Picasso had taught her. Gradually she became a well-known artist herself.

When the picture Picasso gave her was sold, Sylvette had enough money to pay for a beautiful apartment of her very own, with space for a real studio, high on the top floor, with views across the whole of Paris.

Sylvette ran up the stairs. She turned the key – and opened the door . . .

Pablo Picasso was born in Spain in 1881, the son of an art teacher. He could draw before he could speak, and by the time he was twelve he had started to produce astonishingly skillful oil paintings. Throughout his long life his output in every medium was matched only by the extraordinary range of his styles. From delicate etchings to massive and terrifying paintings like *Guernica*, Picasso's work was always pioneering and brutally honest.

Picasso bought a house in Vallauris in the South of France. Here, in 1954, he caught sight of a beautiful, shy teenager, Sylvette David. In a typically frenzied burst of creative energy, Picasso produced more than forty images of "The Girl with a Ponytail," who became an international icon. This was a turbulent time for Picasso. He had recently separated from Françoise Gilot, and met his last wife, Jacqueline Roque, at a pottery in Vallauris. For one summer, Sylvette was Picasso's platonic muse. He always treated her with kindness and respect.

The following year, Picasso had a big exhibition of his "Sylvette" paintings in Paris. Visitors were amazed to see how the work had grown from the first delicate drawing to the sculpture of the girl with a key. But it didn't stop there. A few years later, two concrete sculptures of Sylvette, each as big as a house, were built to Picasso's designs, in Holland and New York.

Picasso produced more than 30,000 original works. He died in 1973, aged 92, one of the most famous artists in the world.

Sylvette David, now Lydia Corbett, lives and paints in the West of England. Her beautiful pictures and wood sculptures can be seen at the Francis Kyle Gallery in London.